BLACKHALL
PAST AND PRESENT

Blackhall 1951 with Craigleith Quarry in the foreground

BLACKHALL PAST AND PRESENT

Over 200 photographs, maps and drawings depicting 150 years in Blackhall

Written and compiled by
Margaret McArthur

ROXBURGH PUBLICATIONS
EDINBURGH

First published in 2000
Roxburgh Publications
Tel: 0131 477 0312
Email: margaret.mcarthur@blueyonder.co.uk

ISBN 0 9526063 2 1

Cover Illustration: Blackhall around 1900

PRINTED IN GREAT BRITAIN
P.E.C BARR PRINTERS LTD, Carron Place, Edinburgh EH6 7RE

BLACKHALL PAST AND PRESENT

CONTENTS

		Page
1	The Village	1
2	Maps	10
3	Ravelston Estate	14
4	Dean Estate	36
5	Barnton Estate	44
6	Craigcrook Estate	77
	Bibliography	120
	Index	121

This book is dedicated to
the memory of
our dear son and friend
George McArthur
who spent most of his 29 years
in Blackhall.

ACKNOWLEDGEMENTS

I would like to thank all the older residents of Blackhall, who have so kindly lent or given me the photographs which has enabled me to produce this book. Many gave them in the past for "Bonnie Blackhall" and I was unable to use them all in that book, so have included them in this one.

Some have more recently been searching through their old photographs and have helped to fill the gaps in my own collection, so I would particularly like to thank Miss J. Orr, Miss H. Stewart and Mr. W. Wood.

I would like to thank Mrs. Scott, headmistress of Blackhall Primary School who gave me the idea of producing a photographic history of the area, when she told me how the smaller children were using "Bonnie Blackhall".

Grateful thanks too to the staff of the Edinburgh Room for the helpful way they provided photographs and information. I would also like to thank the staff of the Royal Commission on the Ancient & Historical Monuments of Scotland, particularly Lesley Ferguson and Anne Lawn Thomas for all their assistance in so many ways and to Iain Drysdale of Mactaggart & Mickel for his enthusiastic help and interest in the project. Thanks too to James Millar & Partners for their help and to local organisations for providing photographs. And further thanks to Margeorie Mekie, a dealer in old picture postcards for introducting me to her collection of Blackhall cards.

And last but by no means least, a big thank-you to my husband, George, for his patience, helpful comments and assistance with proof reading skills.

I have learnt a great deal by studying more closely both the old and recent photographs of Blackhall and I do hope you will enjoy browsing through them.

Margaret McArthur

BLACKHALL VILLAGE

Just when Blackhall came into existence and why it is so named has always been a bit of a puzzle. Stuart Harris in "The Place Names of Edinburgh" states that the 'Black' could derive either from Anglican blaec or Scots blac meaning black and the 'hall' ending is the Anglican 'Halh' or Scots 'Haugh' meaning land beside or in the bend of a river. He goes on to say that "this exactly fits the location upstream from the bridge on the Queensferry Road where the Cottage Park was known as the Haugh in 1770 and Ravelston 1820 shows the fields Whitehall Park and Blackhall Brae". Thus he gives the meaning of the name but it is difficult to envisage the area he is speaking about, particularly as he mentions that there was a Cottage Park on the Ravelston Estate near Craigcrook Castle in another part of his book.

Russel Paton, a resident of Blackhall, writing in the Evening News in 1946 put forward the theory that Blackhall was actually the hamlet known as Clarty Hole in the reign of the Stuarts and that later residents changed the name to Blackhall to make it more 'respectable'

A third theory is that the village took its name from a farm called Blackhall. This arises from mentions in the account book of Sir John Foulis of Ravelston (1680) and Burlaw Court Records from Leith (1741), which both speak of a smith and a court case about hens being allowed to wander on to someone else's ground. However it was 1773 before Blackhall appears on a map (Armstrong's) and even on the map of 1852 (page 10) Blackhall is really only a dot, which makes the farm theory seem the most logical one.

The above is the only known surviving picture of Blackhall village taken around 1865. At that time there were around 50 houses in the village plus sixteen on the estates and the population was about 400. The villagers, in the main, worked on the farms, estates or at the local quarries.

It is thanks to the Denholm family who came to the village in the 1850's that this photograph exists The man in the pony trap is Matthew Denholm, while the figure standing by the cart in white apron and shirt sleeves is his son, Thomas. The village smithy is on the right of the picture and one of the village's blacksmith's was Alexander Denholm. A member of the Denholm family is still living in the village to-day.

The transformation from village to suburb began with the erection in 1884 of Henderson's Buildings or Cottages, pictured above on the left and presumably named after the builder. The picture was taken around 1900 and the one below in 1995. The pend shown in both pictures but most clearly in the lower one once housed the horses, cabs, carts and some of the carters of Tommy Duncan, a well known personality in the village, but is now the premises of the Village Coachworks and Garage.

The village looking north which seems to have been the more favoured view of photographers in the past.   The photograph above was taken around 1900 and shows Henderson's Cottages, House o' Hill Dairy and Hillview Terrace (now Seaforth Terrace) on the right with the tenements of Marischal Place and the Murray Gartshore Hall (the smaller building between the tenements) on the left.   The cottages top left are the Craigcrook Farm Cottages, which lay along the Farm Road, which is now Columba Avenue.

The picture below is of the same period and is entitled 'Edinburgh From Blackhall' but it is difficult to decide precisely from where in Blackhall it was taken.

The tenements that form Marischal Place were completed in 1905 and most have the dates of their completion on them or the initials of the builder.   It became known as Marischal Place in1909 and is named after Alexander Keith of Ravelston House, who was Knighted in 1822 and was a hereditory Earl Marischal of Scotland. The new church of St. Columba's can be seen in the distance on the left.

The sign on the side of Henderson's Cottages in the picture below states that there are 'Villas for Sale first left' and the row of carts may be returning to Craigleith Quarry for further stone to continue building Blackhall.

Queensferry Road, Blackhall.

Above is a much later photograph taken in the 1940's by which time Maidencraig Farm had become a garage. The view is taken from Blinkbonny Crescent and the House O' Hill bungalows can be seen in the far distance. On the police box in the front left of the picture is the siren which was used during the war.

Below shows a similiar view to-day but the small cottage feature in the 40's photograph has gone. It was known as Craggan Cottage and was demolished in 1978.

Craigcrook Terrace and Place were built around 1902 and Denholm Cottage (above left) was built in 1893 but demolished in 1904.

The picture below was taken around 1930 and the small newsagent on the left was Caie's and was responsible for producing many of the sepia postcards which appeared at that time.

The shops were added to Denholm Cottage in 1903, Mr. Alexander Denholm is also featured in the photograph above and his initials are inscribed on the plaques on the walls of the tenement shown below.

Houses continued to be built along both sides of the Queensferry Road. Both these pictures were taken around the same time. Above was probably 1904 as the newly built St. Columba's Church shows up clearly. Below is probably around 1906 as Muirdale Terrace is being erected by Mr. A. Muir, the builder who gave it his name.

QUEENSFERRY ROAD, BLACKHALL.

By the 1930's Blackhall was becoming more recognisable to present inhabitants. The building at the front right of the picture above was once the Blackhall Inn, a staging post and post office before becoming Ware's Stores which was later demolished to be replaced by the Thain Building. The House o' Hill Public House (front right in the picture below) caused quite a stir when built in the late 1930's but has been used by various commercial organisations in recent years

Queensferry Road, Blackhall.

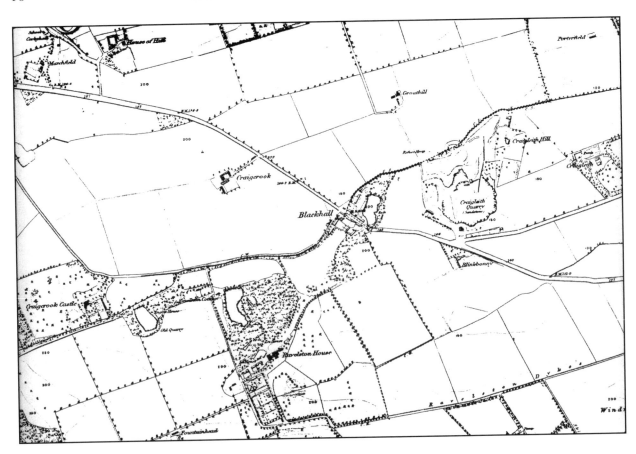

Perhaps maps are even more effective than pictures in showing the change from Blackhall village to Blackhall suburb.   In 1852 (above) the village was really only a dot on the map rating only a slightly larger print than Craigcrook Farm.   Craigcrook Road meandered through the fields of the Craigcrook and Ravelston estates.

By 1896 (below) the railway line had been opened, Craigleith Station built and the village had began to expand along Keith Row and Crescent.

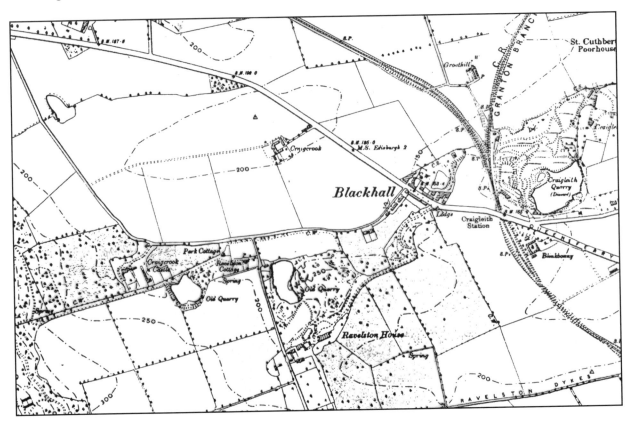

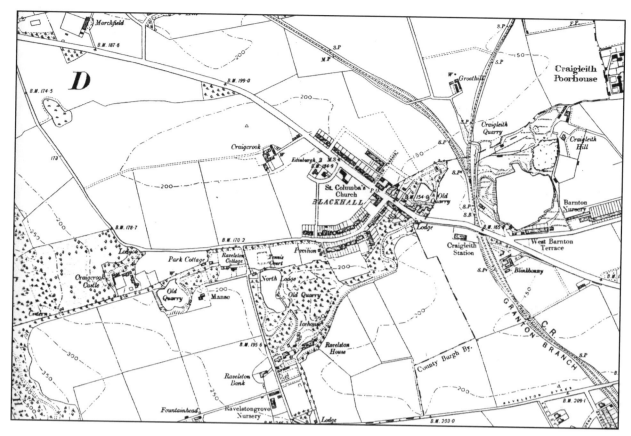

By 1909 (above), villas had been built on the main road and along Craigcrook Road,
Jeffrey Avenue; Barnton Terrace and West Barnton Terrace (now Craigleith Road) had
come into existence and St. Columba's Church had been built.

By 1920 Queen's Avenue, Hillview Terrace (now Seaforth) Forthview Terrace and
Blinkbonny Crescent had been built, and a start made on Columba Road and Gardiner
Road.

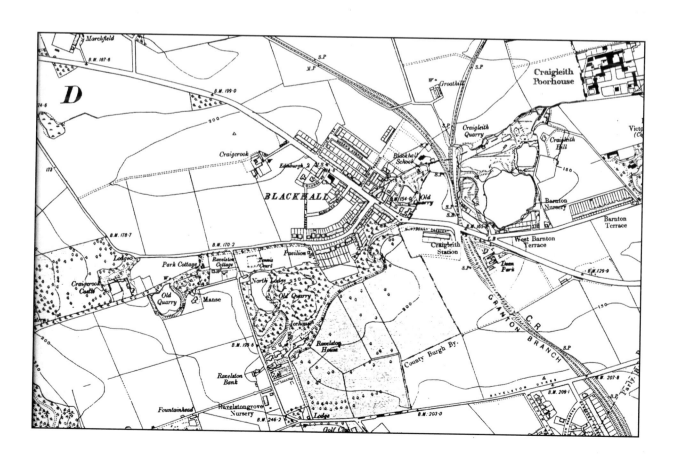

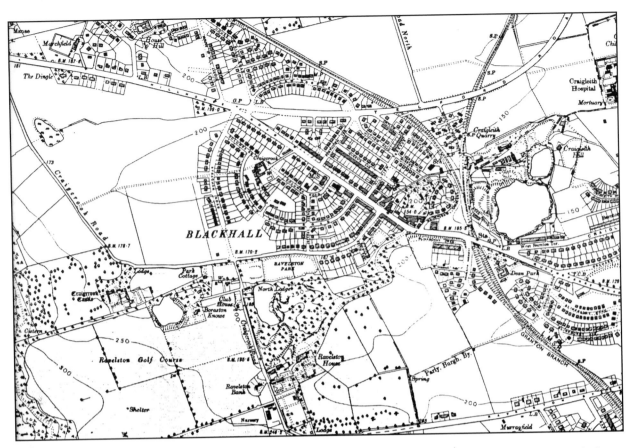

By 1931 (above) Telford Road and Strachan Road had been built with houses being erected along their route, Craigcrook Farm is completely surrounded as Columba Road and Gardiner Road are completed and the Blinkbonny houses continue to appear. And by 1938 (below) the 'bungalow' roads are mapped out but not yet built up. The Ravelston Garden flats have been built but not yet named.

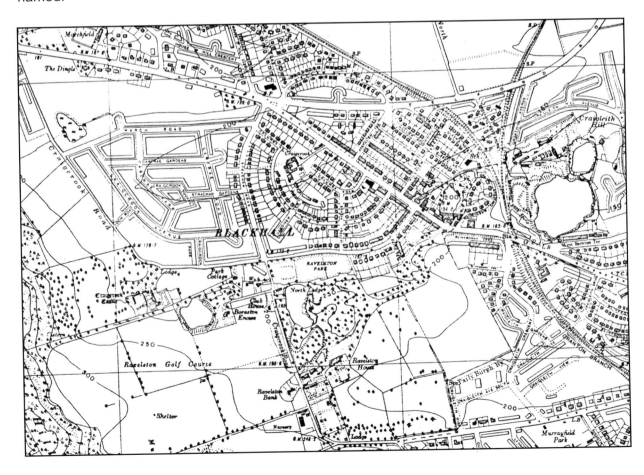

Aerial pictures are also extremely helpful for seeing the changes that have taken place and have the advantage of actually showing buildings. Obviously no aerial pictures exist for the early years of the village, indeed the picture below is probably one of the earliest and is thought to be around 1920.

Drylaw House and Farm can be seen top centre, with a steam train to the right puffing its way to Craigleith Station. Just below the train is Blackhall Primary School built in 1908, and below the trees can be seen the magazine house, where the Keeper of The City of Edinburgh Gunpowder Magazine lived. Seaforth Terrace (Hillview Terrace at that time) is in the process of being built as is Gardiner Road. The plots of land along Gardiner Road were allotments which were used during the First World War for growing extra food supplies. St. Columba's Church is the large building centre left of the picture with the smaller first church building to the rear of it. This building was used as the church hall until the 1950's.

The village of Blackhall had the misfortune of being trisected by the parish boundaries of the churches of Cramond, Corstorphine and St. Cuthbert's originally but latterly Dean replaced St. Cuthbert's. It was also trisected by the boundaries of three estates - Ravelston, Craigcrook and Drylaw, but Drylaw was later swallowed up by the Barnton estate of which some parts were later sold, but at the time of the development of Blackhall much of it was owned by the Steel-Maitlands. The Queensferry Road was the boundary between the Steel Maitland Estate and Craigcrook and Ravelston, with Craigcrook Road forming the boundary between Ravelston and Craigcrook until just before Craigcrook Castle when the land on both sides of the road belonged to the Craigcrook estate. Indeed the Craigcrook estate went over the hill to Clermiston, with March Road forming the boundary between it and the Steel Maitland estate. As the suburb developed, it also encroached on to the Dean Estate. The estates developed in different ways for various reasons and it is these differences that we will be looking at in the following pages beginning with the Ravelston Estate.

The Murray Gartshore Memorial Hall was built in 1885 by Miss Murray Gartshore in memory of her father. Initially the hall served the community as the church, school, bank and recreation hall. This moonlit picture was featured on the cover of The Rec Magazines of 1918 & 1919 and shows a man entering the hall. By 1908 a church and school had been built and Miss Murray Gartshore handed over the management of the Hall to a newly formed Blackhall Recreation Association and gave a substantial donation to equiping the hall with a billiard table and bowling rink, plus 50 books with which to start a library. A further extension to the hall was made in 1913 and a full sized billiard table was purchased due to popular demand. Miss Murray Gartshore died in 1915 and it was

found that she had bequeathed the hall and premises upstairs in trust for the benefit of the community of Blackhall. The hall continued to be used for recreational purposes until 1968 when it closed due to lack of members. It then served the community as a small supermarket for several years and has been used by a variety of different commercial organisations since. Below the recreational hall in the early 1990's

Ravelston Lodge, pictured above, was demolished shortly after the other cottages which had made up Blackhall village and was replaced by the new lodge around 1900 although the picture below was taken in the 1990's.

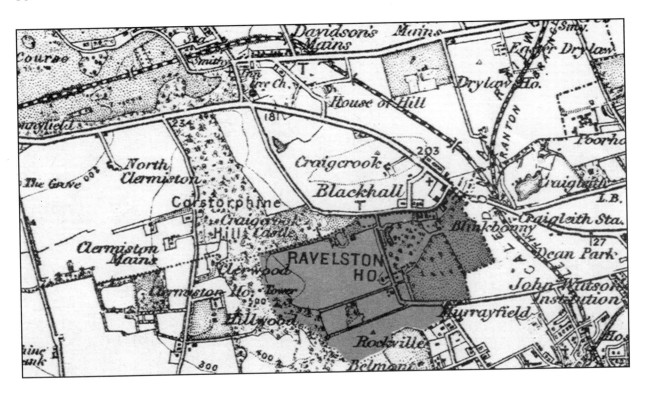

The above map is part of the Key Map included in the sales brochure when Ravelston Estate was sold after the death of Miss Murray Gartshore in 1915. It gives some idea as to the area of Blackhall it actually covered and indeed how large it was. It consisted of some 283 acres and included the Bowling and Tennis Club, the Park, both Murrayfield and Ravelston Golf Clubs, part of Corstorphine Woods as far as the Rest and Be Thankful plus Marischal Place, Keith Row, Terrace and Crescent.

Below is one of the pictures also included in the sales brochure and shows what the house, gardens and grounds looked like in 1915.

Ravelston Estate dates back to 1363 when it was part of the barony of Dean and was donated to "a chaplain in the church of St. Giles" by Sir William More of Abercorn. In 1620 the estate came into the posession of George Foulis, who built the first Ravelston House. Unfortunately around 1835 it was burnt down, leaving only the north wing which was converted into a house for the head gardener and steward (pictured above)

The doorway below is part of the above house and although George Foulis' initials have been covered by ivy, his initials and the date 1622 plus the initials of his second wife, Janet Bannatyne are above the door. The tall staircase tower pictured below left also dates back to that early period.

This house was built about 1837 and contained on the ground floor a large entrance hall, four public rooms, a cloakroom, butler's pantry, 3 servants rooms and a store room.   On the first floor there were six bedrooms, plus a dressing room and 3 servants rooms.   And the top floor contained a billiard room, a photographic dark room plus three further bedrooms. And in the basement was the kitchen, numerous stores, the servants hall, the housekeeper's bedroom, the butler's bedroom and the wine cellar.   Outside in the yard was a dairy and in the adjoining building a Sawmill and Workshop.   There were also two stable blocks and a coachhouse or garage and a coachman's house.

The ornamental gardens covered one acre and were open to the public once a year and the proceeds given to charity. The kitchen garden covered three acres.

To continue the story of the Ravleston Estate.   George Foulis died in 1633 and was succeeded by his son John, in whose account book was the first mention of Blackhall.   In 1661 he married Margaret, daughter of Sir Alexander Primrose and Ravelston continued to be held by his descendents until 1726 when Sir Archibald Primrose sold it to Alexander Keith W.S.   The Keiths were a famous Scottish family and gave their name to several streets in the area.   Sir Walter Scott was a relative of the family and a frequent visitor to Ravelston.   In 1873 Sir. Patrick Keith Murray sold the estate to his uncle Colonel Murray Gartshore and in due time it passed to his daughter Miss Mary Anne Georgina Murray Gartshore, pictured below standing standing by a fountain bearing the date 1630 which was removed to Wemyss Castle in 1961.

Miss Murray Gartshore took a very matriachal interest in the village of Blackhall at the turn of the century. As well as having the Recreational Hall (see page 14) built in memory of her father and providing it with books and equipment, she also feu-leased much of the estate land to provide further amenities for the community.   Whether the initiative for these ventures came from Miss Murray Gartshore or the community is not clear, but she appears to have been involved in most of the developments which have certainly been of benefit to the community of to-day.

Reproduced by kind permission of Murrayfield Golf Club

The first of these amenities was Murrayfield Golf Club which was founded in 1896 and expanded in 1903 and the above photograph shows Sir Lewis and Lady McIver driving off at the opening of the expanded course.   Miss Murray Gartshore insisted on the right of free golf for herself and her guests and there was to be no golf on Sundays.

Two years later Blackhall Bowling Club was formed initially on the site of the present day Tennis Club, but moved to its present site in 1913.   The picture below shows what looks like the whole community turning out to one of the events.   The recreation hall can be seen in the background with the little bell tower, which used to call people to worship, children to school and savers to the penny bank.

Ravelston Golf Club became a a limited company on the 11th October 1912 and aroused such local interest that the official photographer had difficulty in getting everyone in the photograph above.   Below shows the 14 directors of the newly formed company.

The Tennis Club was formed in 1915 taking over the site and club house which had been previously occupied by the Bowling Club.

What the initial arrangements were with regard to Ravelston Park are unclear but the Blackhall Sports appear to have started in 1909 and continues to be popular to the present day, although the two photographs show just how much they have changed in character over the years.   What has not changed is that it is still very much a community event.

Miss Murray Gartshore arranged other events for the young people of the area, this picnic in Ravelston Woods was organised to celebrate the coronation of Kirk GeorgeV and Queen Mary in 1911. Miss Murray Gartshore died in 1915 and it was her successor at Ravelston House, Mrs. Stewart Clark, who provided the football strip for the Blackhall Athletic Lads and allowed them to use Ravelston Park as their ground. The photograph below was taken about 1932/33 after the final of the Lothian Amateur Football Association when the Athletic Lads had defeated Leith Celtic by 3 goals to 1

Mrs. Stewart Clark died in 1959 and bequeathed Ravelston House to the Church of Scotland to be used as an Eventide Home, and the gardens to Edinburgh Corporation. However, the death duties on the estate were so high that neither the Church or the Corporation felt able to accept the terms and the estate was sold to T. Boland & Company Ltd., who then sold 35 acres of it to the Edinburgh Merchant Company for the Mary Erskine School for Girls. Thus the house and grounds of Ravelston changed greatly during the 20th century. Above as it was in 1915 below as it looks to-day.

Similar changes also occurred in the village part of the estate. Above is Keith Row at the time of a fire in Simpson's Dairy around 1898, Keith Row having been built in 1896 and named after the Keiths of Ravelston.
Below is is the same view in 1995 showing Keith Row and Craigcrook Place and how the the main road also looks quite different with the shops and tenement flats

The large house, known as the Grove, seen in the picture above at the end of Keith Row had to be taken down because of subsidence and was replaced by a modern bungalow and for some time there was a building occupied by Rentokil but in the 1990's it was also demolished and replaced by the modern flats seen in the picture below

Above - a closer view of the flats.
Below - Keith Terrace showing signs of the subsidence which affected the other houses, but which now appears to be stable.

Ravelston Park is used by children of all ages, the swing park being popular with the younger children and the grassy area with the footballers. There are now two exit points into Ravelston Woods.

Below shows the Park Pavillion which was recently converted to form Blackhall Nursery, where 24 under fives meet for the morning session and a further 24 come along in the afternoon.

For many years the field next to Ravelston Park was known as the Scout Field as the local Scout Troop had their Scout Hut there and made use of the field. Also for a number of years, the PTA of Blackhall Primary School held Bonfire Night celebrations in the field, the Scouts allowing the hut to be used for hot soup and rolls - always welcome on a cold November night.

However in 1998 Cala Homes (Scotland) Ltd. were given planning permission to build on the field four luxury houses each with five bedrooms, an integral conservatory and double garage. Above the building in progress and below the field as it now looks.

The Ravelston Quarries were the oldest in the area, being first mentioned in 1511 and the first Ravelston House is said to have been completely built with stone from these quarries. The remains of all four are still visible to-day, two in the region of Murrayfield Golf Club, one behind Blackhall School (pictured below) and the other lies behind the Cala Homes in Craigcrook Road (pictured above in 1995). Although there were several periods of inactivity, the quarries became active again at the beginning of the 20th century and the stone was used for buildings in the Blackhall area until 1939.

The shops at the corner of Ravleston Dykes Road and Craigcrook Road were built in the late thirties and the houses on that corner in the early forties.

The above picture of Park Cottage (75 Craigcrook Road) was taken from Ravelston Estate in 1915 for the sale brochure. The cottage was built around 1850 and may have been designed by Playfair, who was working on Craigcrook Castle at the time.   When it went up for sale around 1980, it was described as a quite delightful cottage style house consisting 3 public rooms, 5 bedrooms and in need of general modernisation.The ground extended to one and a half acres with tennis lawn, tennis pavillion, garage, outhouses including a concrete air-raid shelter and a spinney.   Offers over £95,000 were invited.
Below shows the house as viewed from Craigcrook Road.

The advertisment had also stated that the property could have considerable development potential and as can be seen from above it was this development potential which was realised and the Cottage Park Housing Complex was designed and built.   Below, Cottage Park as it looks to-day.

© *British Crown Copyright/MOD*

The above is a picture of Blinkbonny Farm taken from Ravelston Dykes and showing the extent of its fields. It was on the Dean Estate. Craigleith Station can just be made out in the centre of the picture to the left of the farm, with the old railway line running from it and out to the right of the photograph. Just how old the farm was is unknown but it is featured on Armstrong's map of 1773. Sometime between 1909 and 1920 Blinkbonny Farm became Dean Park and house building in its immediate area greatly increased as the 1951 aerial picture left shows. The farm is in the middle of the trees and Craigleith Station can just be seen at the corner of the Queensferry Road and Craigleith Crescent.

Dean Park was probably demolished in the early 60's and was replaced by the Crest Hotel, designed by Morris and Steedman and built in 1968. The Hotel has changed hands on more than one occasion and is now the Holiday Inn, pictured above, and a well known local landmark.

Below The Esso Garage now stands on what was the entrance to Dean Park.

Some of the streets in the area took their names from the farm - Blinkbonny is a reversal of bonnie blink meaning a fine view.
Blinkbonny Crescent above and below as it is to-day was built in 1905.

James Millar and Son and local builder C.H. Dunlop built many of the Blinkbonny houses. Above is the first of the Millar houses built in the 1930's and below is an aerial view of the Blinkbonny housing taken in 1991. The road at the top of the picture is the Queensferry Road passing through Orchard Park and the road at the bottom is Ravelston Dykes.

Crown Copyright: Royal Commission on the Ancient & Historical Monuments of Scotland

This 1930's post card states that this is Blinkbonny Avenue, but Daniel Stewart's College, as it was then, cannot be seen from Blinkbonny Crescent and the road is actually Belford Gardens, which was built in 1932 and took its name from Belford Road.

Blinkbonny Avenue, Blackhall.

Left
A slightly leafier
Belford Gardens
as it is to-day

Right
Blinkbonny Avenue
was built in 1926
but this photograph
of it was taken in
2000.

Left
Blinkbonny Road
as it is to-day. It
was built in 1928.

Right
Blinkbonny
Terrace pictured
in the 1930's
shortly after it
was built in 1926

Blinkbonny Terrace, Blackhall.

Left
Blinkbonny Terrace
as it is to-day

Craigleith Station, pictured above, had a comparatively short life but a very busy one. Opened for passenger trains in 1879, the railway line was a busy commuter line not only for Blackhall residents but for those from Barnton and Granton.   However as bus services improved, the station became less busy and was finally closed and demolished in the early sixties.   In the picture below of the present day cycle track, the platform is still clearly visible although the bridge is almost hidden by the trees.

The station along with the neighbouring roads called Craigleith took their name from Craigleith Quarry, which in turn was named after an estate dating back to 1171 Crag of Inverleith, crag meaning hill.
Craigleith Crescent above was built in 1926 and Craigleith Drive below in 1928.

CRAIGLEITH QUARRY

Local quarries supplied the stone for many houses in Blackhall, but the quarries were, in fact, almost worked out by 1900.   Craigleith is the largest and best known of the quarries and dates back to 1615 when it was known as Enderleith or Innerleith, and over the centuries has produced stone for Edinburgh Castle, the University, the National Monument on CaltonHill and Buckingham Palace.   It was at its busiest during the building of the New Town.

The quarry was reputed to be 360 feet deep and even after its 'hey-day' was past, it was still recorded as being 200 feet deep and covering 7 acres in 1892. Above is Shepherd's Engraving of the quarry in 1829. By 1905 only 25 workers were employed at the quarry and the stone used mainly for rubble work. During the First World War, the Lothian Chemical Company manufactured T.N.T. in the quarry, but after the war quarrying began again but employed very few men and finally stopped in 1941-42.

Below is a later view of the quarry when it had become flooded.

The above photocopy of an aerial picture taken during the 1930's is rather blurred but it does show just how big an area the Quarry covered even at that time. The picture is taken from the north with the junction of Telford Road and Queensferry Road at the bottom centre of the picture. By following the line of the Queensferry Road to its junction with Craigleith Road, it is possible to make out the huge mass of Craigleith Quarry towards the top left of the picture.

© British Crown Copyright/MOD.

Above, is another aerial view taken in 1951 and from a different viewpoint. This time we are looking towards Blackhall and the houses of Groathill and Maidencraig can be clearly seen. By looking at this picture one can understand why parents warned children to stay away from the quarry and why there were several accidents there over the years.

Gradually the quarry was filled in and below it is seen being prepared for the building of Sainsbury's Superstore in 1995

AN AERIAL VIEW OF THE CRAIGLEITH QUARRY SITE IN 1995

This picture is already out of date as the top part of the quarry site is now occupied by the Craigleith Shopping Centre containing Homebase, Curries, Boots and Textile World to name but a few.   The large Sainsbury Superstore and car park can be clearly seen in the centre of the photograph

Since being built in 1995, Sainsbury Superstore has been enlarged to include many new departments. It is pictured above across the car park and shows some of the landscaping which was included in the development.
Below the Craigleith Centre also pictured across the car park.

The shops and flats at the corner of Craigleith Road and Groathill Road South (pictured above) had to be demolished in order to make a car entrance into Sainsbury's Superstore.

Below shows what that corner looks like to-day.

The back of Craigleith Road is seen in the picture above with the crags of the Quarry in the foreground. When the first houses were built in 1885 they were called, somewhat confusingly, West Barnton Terrace and Barnton Terrace, but in 1968 the whole road became unified as Craigleith Road.

Below shows Craigleith Road as it is to-day.

Baillie's Advertising pictured above was once known fondly by the residents of Blackhall as the 'Store'.   St. Cuthbert's Cooperative Society built the Blackhall Emporium in 1928 and it also included the shops pictured below and had a wide range of departments - grocery, butcher, tailoring, furniture and furnishings and boot and shoe to name only a few. The war years brought problems and by 1945 it was no longer an Emporium but 4 individual shops.   In 1957 Nos 160 and 161 were demolished and further reorganisation took place in 1968 but all to no avail and the 'Store' finally closed in the 1980's.

In 1939 planning permission was being sought to build a cinema to seat 2000 people in the area above, but by the end of the war it was decided that housing was more necessary than a cinema and Maidencraig Court was built in 1955.

Maidencraig Farm, below, became a garage about 1937, when the farmer, Mr. Wood, found that the city folk moving out to the area did not like the 'country smells' of the animals and increasing public health regulations made it impossible to keep going. Coverting it to a garage did retain the farm buildings, some of the very few to survive in the area, however the garage was sold in 1998 and just what is going to happen to the buildings now is not known.

Maidencraig Quarry was a small quarry but was also of ancient origin, dating back to 1628, when it provided stone for Edinburgh Castle, and later for the North Bridge. However by 1853 the quarry was flooded and probably abandoned. The building in the picture above was used for many years as a Gunpowder Magazine Store and in the 1890's the Keeper of the Magazine was a gentleman by the name of Robert Burns, great grandson of Scotland's national bard. The aerial picture below shows that by 1951 the quarry had been filled in, the north side of Maidencraig Crescent had yet to be built - the only house standing was demolished in 1998 and replaced by a modern bungalow.

© *British Crown Copyright/MOD*

In 1982 Viewpoint Housing Association began building a sheltered housing development providing accommodation for 48 elderly people - 24 one person flats and 12 flats for couples - on part of the old quarry site.
Below the Sheltered Housing Development as it is to-day.

The above was taken from an ancient photocopy of Maidencraig Villa, owned by James Simpson, with the buildings of House o' Hill Dairy on either side, but the dairy was much more commonly known as Simpson's Dairy.   It dates back to the 1890's and was a well known landmark.

The dairy buildings on the left above are shown below as they are to-day and now occupied by different commercial enterprises.

The above picture of a fire at the dairy was taken from Keith Row in the late 1890's. The dairy was reputed to have accommodation for well over 100 cows and it is said that when the dairy foreman roused the milkmaids for the morning milking, he also managed to awaken half of the village. The picture below shows the dairy in better times and just how it fitted into the village at that time.

4085 Seaforth Ter

An even later view of the dairy is pictured above, probably sometime in the late 1930's as it was demolished in the 40's to make way for the shops and flats featured in the photograph below taken in 1995 and showing how that side of the village has changed.

Seaforth Drive was built around 1900 and was originally named Hillview Terrace but was renamed in 1967, as was Hillview Road which became Forthview Drive, to prevent confusion with the Corstorphine Hillviews.

The houses shown below were the first ones to be built.

Queen's Avenue was built in the early 1900's and there is debate as to whether it was called after Queen Victoria or Queen Alexandra.   Above shows the avenue when half built and below shows it as it looks to-day.

Above - Queen's Avenue in the 1930's - the photographer, who took these sepia postcards, seems to have a liking for children in his photographs as he uses children in a number of them.
Below a similar view to-day.

Queen's Avenue South was also built in the early 1900's and was originally called Hillview Crescent and was also renamed in 1968.

Queen's Road is of slightly later origin being built around 1923.
Both the above pictures show the roads as they are to-day.

Above Queen's Road in the 1930's with some more small children on hand but this was not surprising in this road as at that time, it led down to Blackhall Primary School . Below the same view to-day with hedges and trees intervening.

The Blackhall School Logbook begins in October 1902 when the school met in the Recreational Hall and 37 children attended, with older children taking the longer walk over to Roseburn Primary.   However, with the community expanding, Cramond School Board decided that a new school building was required and in 1908 the children moved into their new school, which won a prize for its architect John Watson.   Above the new school sometime after 1923 as Queen's Crescent can be seen in the background.

Above the old school as it looked in 1979 after its closure.

Flowering Cherry Trees were planted by the children in 1954 and softened the outline of the building, but as the community continued to expand, the school was soon overcrowed and various huts were erected in the playground as can be seen in the picture below, again taken after the school's closure. By the 1960's the overcrowding problems had become acute, the room intended for a gym hall was being used as a classroom and the children had to eat their school dinners in the corridor.

The old school was finally closed in 1979 and demolished in December 1989 and was replaced by a sheltered housing development of some 55 flats for the elderly, built by McCarthy and Stone and named Queen's Court.

A new Blackhall Primary School was built in Craigcrook Road (pictured above) and was opened in 1979. Unfortunately the rate of expansion in the community was again underestimated and temporary huts have had to be built in the playground (pictured below) and the gymn hall is too small for the whole school to gather together for an assembly or school concerts. However there are plans to rectify this situation

Forthview Terrace, Blackhall.   M. 110.

Forthview Terrace was built and named around 1904, probably because of the glimpse of the Firth of Forth it had until the land was built up to the north east.
Above shows how it looked in the 1930's and below how it looks to-day.
Prior to 1968 Forthview Road was named Hillview Road.

Drylaw Crescent was also built in the early thirties and was named after the estate of Drylaw at the suggestion of W.C. Davidson who was factor of the estate at that time. Again the above picture was taken in the late thirties or early forties and the picture below is as the crescent looks to-day.

Telford Road, Blackhall.

Telford Road was built in 1929 and named after the great engineer Thomas Telford. It improved the route, from Leith to Queensferry and, via Maybury to Glasgow.
The above picture is possibly around 1940 and the picture below (2000) shows the alterations which were made after the completion of the buildings.

The House o' Hill houses took took their name from the farm in that area and were in the main built around 1932/33.

Above shows House O' Hill Avenue in the late 30's early 40's and below the avenue as it is to-day.

Blackhall United Free Church began life in an empty shop across the road from its present site (the launderette to be precise) and the first service was held there on the 14th January 1934.   The Memorial Stone of the building was unveiled on 12th October, 1935 by Mrs. Forrestor-Paton and the new hall opened on 29th February 1936 by Mrs. William Dunn.   Due to the enthusiasm and hard work of the office bearers and congregation, an extension was added to the building on 31st May, 1969 which made it possible for the congregation to have a permanently furnished church.

The shops and flats above were built in the late 1930's whereas the Hillhouse shops below did not go up until the 1940's.

Hillview, Blackhall.   M. 110

Hillview was built around 1900 and named in that year and at that time there was no doubt a clear view of Corstorphine Hill. Above shows the road as it looked in the thirties and below as it looks to-day.

Telford Road, Blackhall.

The above picture was possibly taken in the early 1940's for although the Whitehall Garage is shown on the 1938 map, it is not named and the shops and flats are not shown on the map at all.
Below the same view to-day.

BLACKHALL LIBRARY

The first Blackhall Library was opened in the Murray Gartshore Memorial Hall in the village in 1909 (see page14). However in 1948 Edinburgh City Libraries opened a Blackhall branch (pictured right). This proved to be so popular that plans were soon afoot to replace the temporary building with a much larger library.

The present library (pictured below) was designed by architects Bradshaw, Gass and Hope and features an attractive central garden courtyard containing a pool and seats which may be used by readers on suitable days. It was opened on 21st March 1966 and in addition to the lending service, there were reference and junior sections plus a discussion room. In the first six months there was an overall increase in book issues of 68%. Various other services have been added over the years and the library has gone on from strength to strength.

The above pictures are reproduced by kind permission of Edinburgh City Libraries

Hillhouse Road, sections of which are seen above and below. The name of the road dates from 1927 and is based on House O' Hill.

Above is the more recent section which was built in 1824 as part of the new Queensferry Turnpike which went on an entirely new line through Marchfield and King's Cramond.

The section below is part of the old Queensferry Road which carried straight on by Corbiehill to Muttonhole. The top section was on the Barton Estate and the bottom section on the Craigcrook Estate.

Craigcrook Farm, the large building on the left above, was one of the oldest farms in the area dating back to the 1360's. The lands were originally owned by a family called Graham who donated them to John De Alyncrum, a Burgess of Edinburgh, who in turn settled the income from the land on a Chaplaincy at St. Giles. In 1376 the lands were let in feu to Patrick and John Leper. The above picture was taken around 1903, when surburbia was already beginning to creep up on it. The present St. Columba's Church was being built (top right) at that time which makes it possible to date the picture. Below shows the farm at an earlier date with the farmer hard at work in his fields.

It is difficult now to envisage this view (above) looking down towards Craigcrook Road and Ravelston Woods. Below is a picture of Craigcrook Farm from a bungalow in Gardiner Road in the late 1930's just before the farm was demolished in the early 1940's.

The above aerial picture taken in the late 1930's is not of the best quality but it is clear enough to recognise certain landmarks. The road intersection in the centre at the foot of the photograph is the Telford Road/ Queensferry Road/ Strachan Road junction, some houses have been built in Columba Road but Craigcrook Farm is still dividing the road although now almost completely surrounded by bungalows. The mist in the background shows why Edinburgh had the nickname at one time of Auld Reekie.

As previously mentioned, the lands of Craigcrook date back to 1362 but were centred around Craigcrook Farm and remained so until 1542 when William Adamson was assigned the estate in perpetual feu farm and heritage. This gentleman had considerable property extending from Craigleith to Cammo. Craigcrook Castle was built in 1545 and the estate continued to pass to heirs until 1656 when Robert Adamson broke up the large estate and sold it to different people. Craigcrook passed through several hands until it was bought by John Strachan W.S. in 1698. When he died in 1719 he left the whole of the estate plus most of his fortune for charitable purposes - the Craigcrook Mortification Trust. The income from the estate was to be given to poor old men and women and orphans, which continues to the present day when there are about 31 pensioners on the books each receiving £500. per annum.

At the beginning of the 19th century the castle was leased to the publisher, Archibald Constable, who made considerable improvements to the Castle and grounds.   It was in 1815 that Lord Jeffrey came to live at the castle and spent 35 seasons there.   He was an advocate and became Lord Advocate and Member of Parliament for Edinburgh.   He also edited the Edinburgh Review and Craigcrook became a centre for literary and political discussion.   He died in 1850 and the next occupant of the castle was John Hunter, son of Professor Hunter of St. Andrew's, who was followed in 1874 by the Croall family who occupied the castle until 1966. It is now used by various commercial companies.

Naturally the commercial enterprises operating within the Castle had to extend the premises to make them more 'user friendly' and the above buildings were added but the Castle still retains in the main its previous grandeur.

The flower and vegetable gardens plus the greenhouses and vinery have all gone as have the putting green and tennis court, but the adjacent park lands continue to provide a beautiful view from the Castle

As with Ravelston Estate Lodge in the village, the old Craigcrook Lodge was demolished and replaced by a much more modern house.

1926 must have been a very busy year in this particular part of Blackhall, for Craigcrook Park, pictured above, and Craigcrook Avenue, pictured below plus Craigcrook Grove and Square were all built in that year.

Strachan Road was built in 1926 and the picture above was probably taken in the thirties and shows it looking strangely different to the tree lined street it is to-day (pictured below). Strachan Road was named after John Strachan W.S., the last owner of the Craigcrook Estate (see page 81).

Strachan Gardens was built in 1931 and Strachan House, a nursing home for up to 90 residents in Craigcrook Road was opened in 1996.

Carfrae Road (pictured above) and Carfrae Park and Grove were all built in 1926 but Crafrae Gardens (pictured below) was of a slightly later vintage, namely 1931.   These streets were name after the senior partner of Carfrae & Morrison, civil engineers, who laid out the estate roads for the Craigcrook Mortification Trust

March Road, Blackhall.

The picture above was probably taken in the early 1930's shortly after the road was built in 1926. "March" means the boundary line of property and was in this case the boundary of the Craigcrook Estate and farm. March Road, where it joins Strachan Road, has not changed greatly over the years apart from a growth in hedges, trees and cars.

There was bad flooding in the Jeffrey Avenue area in 1927 just 3 years after it had been built in1924. The road was named after Lord Jeffrey, one of Craigcrook Castle's most famous tenants.

Right
In the
1930's

Left
In the
1940's

Right
In 2000

Gardiner Road, Blackhall.

Gardiner Road was started in 1921 and was named after the Rev. Dr. Gardiner, Minister of Kirknewton and chairman of the Craigcrook Mortification Trust. Gardiner Grove and Terrace were built in 1931 and 1932.

Above shows Gardiner Road in the 1930's and below as it is to-day.

Some housing was built in Columba Road shortly after the St. Columba's present church building was erected in 1904, the road was further extended in 1926 when it was named after the church but not fully completed until Craigcrook Farm was demolished in the early 1940's.

The above view is in the thirties and the picture below was taken in 2000.

Above the completed Columba Road as it looks to-day.
Below Columba Avenue, which was built on the old farm road and named in 1936.

The church of St. Columba's was built due to the foresight of the minister of Cramond Church, who noted the amount of building that was going on in the Blackhall area and, as part of it fell within the parish of Cramond, he approached the other churches responsible

for the area - Dean and Corstorphine - and the Edinburgh Presbytery and it was agreed to build a church, which was opened on the 4th of March 1900. Unfortunately there are no pictures of this first church building on its own, but it is the smaller of the two buildings in the picture above.

The new congregation, however, quickly realised that this building was not going to be large enough to meet their needs and, under the leadership of their minister, Rev. W. B. Stevenson, they set to work to raise the money for a new church building.

Mr. P. McGregor Chalmers was appointed as architect and produced this artisitic impression (left) of the church he planned for the area. Whether he changed his plans or the congregation decided against the tall tower and steeple is unclear but it was certainly never built.

The foundation stone for the new building was laid in 1903 for which the residents of the village turned out in force. The building was completed in 1904 and the church dedicated and opened for worship on the 28th May of that year.

The population of Blackhall continued to grow and thirty years later, St. Columba's again had problems accommodating all its members and an extension which would seat a further 450 was added to the church bringing the total seating seating capacity up to 940. A Session Room was included in the extension and is now used as the church office.

Besides giving extra seating, the extension also greatly changed the look of the interior of the church, making it much larger and brighter and necessitating that the pulpit should be moved from the right hand side of the church to the left hand side, so that members in the new gallery and south aisle were also able to see the preacher.   The picture above was taken in the 1930's prior to the extension being built and the one below when the church was decorated for Christmas in 1949.

Above - The church as it is to-day.

Below - the chapel in the North Aisle showing the original font.

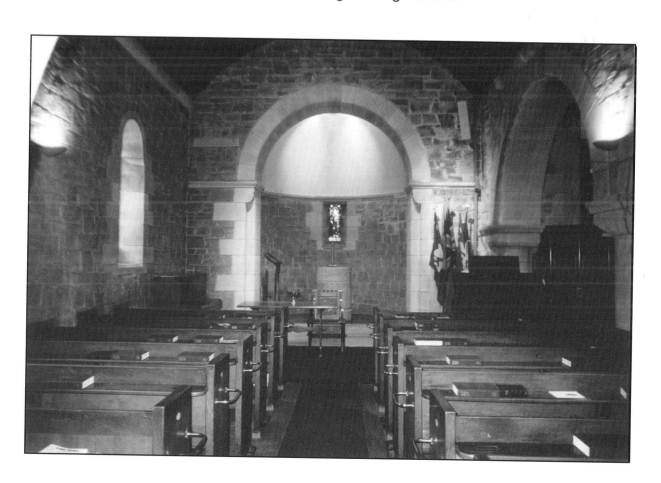

The original church building was used as the church hall until the 1950's when it was demolished to make room for a new set of halls which were opened in 1957, and an upper extension was added to the halls in 1978 to meet the increasing needs of the church and community.   The picture below shows the halls as they are in 2000.

Craigcrook Place and Terrace were both erected around 1903 and are pictured above in the 1990's.

Below - Craigcrook Place in the early thirties when Simpson's Dairy was still in existence at the end of the road.

Craigcrook Gardens, pictured above, are upper and lower villa flats and were also built in 1903 but were unfortunately affected by subsidence and the houses which originally completed Craigcrook Gardens had to be taken down. These were replaced by the more modern houses pictured below.

The villas in the first part of Craigcrook Road and Keith Crescent were all built around 1900 and were some of the first houses in the new 'garden surburb' of Blackhall.

Craigcrook Road, Blackhall.

As already noted when looking at the maps, the bungalows were not built until the 1930's and apart from a steady growth in the trees, have not changed much as can be seen by comparing the two pictures on this page.

A change in the style of houses occurred very briefly (above) before returning to the traditional bungalows below.

In the late thirties, the view at the end of March Road looking across Craigcrook Road to Corstorphine Hill was as above.

Below is the Marle Pits, which to many in the area is only a name from the past. This view was also taken from March Road, near the end of Craigcrook Avenue; the road running across the centre of the picture depicted by hedging is Craigcrook Road and the houses which can just be seen in the distance were the first of the Mactaggart & Mickel houses to be built on the Queensferry Road. It was this stretch of water which gave rise to the northern section of Craigcrook Road being known as Loch Road locally.

HILLPARK ESTATE

OVERLOOKING THE BEAUTIFUL WOODLANDS OF DAVIDSON'S MAINS & CORSTORPHINE HILL PARKS. THE FINEST RESIDENTIAL DISTRICT IN EDINBURGH, YET ONLY 12 MINUTES FROM PRINCES STREET.

This picturesque estate in the Queensferry Road has been chosen as the site for a limited number of distinguished Bungalows and Villas. Each design has been prepared with due regard to the amenities of its setting and the architecture is dignified and practical. Every house has a charming aspect and many have an uninterrupted vista of magnificent parkland.

The above illustration shows a 5-apartment Bungalow for which the price is £1100. There are also other types of houses ranging in price from £900. Prices include road charges.

Show Houses are now open daily (including Sundays) from 1 p.m. until dusk and inspection is cordially invited.

HOW TO GET THERE. S.M.T. or Corporation 'Buses from Hope Street Post Office (West End) to Craigcrook Road or Davidson's Mains Cross respectively. Trains from Caledonian Station (L.M.S.) to Davidson's Mains.

Mactaggart & Mickel Ltd

67 YORK PLACE - - - - - - EDINBURGH
TELEPHONE — EDINBURGH 21717

Crown Copyright: Royal Commission on the Ancient and Historical Momuments of Scotland

The above 1937 advertisment gave details of the new Hillpark Estate to the general public

Crown Copyright: Royal Commission on the Ancient and Historical Momuments of Scotland

The finalised plan by Stewart Kaye envisaged 78 plots arranged along the Queensferry Road (pictured above with not a car to be seen!) and Craigcrook Road, plus along Hillpark Avenue and two smaller roads.   The first sale was in March 1936 of 409 Queensferry Road - a 6 apartment detached villa with garage was sold for £1,485 with a down payment of £75.   Sales plummeted in 1939 with the threat of war but 51 of the houses had been sold by 1941.

Below shows that the view from Queensferry Road at that point was also quite different although the old telephone exchange at the end of Craigcrook Road is still clearly recognisable

Crown Copyright: Royal Commission on the Ancient and Historical Momuments of Scotland

Crown Copyright: Royal Commission on the Ancient and Historical Momuments of Scotland

The pictures above and below give some idea of why the estate was called Hillpark with the amount of meadow land and woods around it must indeed have seemed like living in the country.

Crown Copyright: Royal Commission on the Ancient and Historical Momuments of Scotland

Crown Copyright: Royal Commission on the Ancient and Historical Momuments of Scotland

After the war sales increased again and between 1947 and 1958 over 300 houses were built on the estate although by that time a five apartment detached house in Hillpark Avenue cost £3,550.

Crown Copyright: Royal Commission on the Ancient and Historical Momuments of Scotland

Hillpark Avenue (above) certainly looks very different to-day to what it did in those early days (opposite top picture)

The house building expanded to cover the fields below the Queensferry Road and was named as a continuation of Craigcrook Road although, as can be seen below, built in a slightly different style

Crown Copyright: Royal Commission on the Ancient and Historical Momuments of Scotland

As Craigcrook Road was extended on the one side, houses were also built on the Corstorphine Hill side of the Craigcrook Road.

Crown Copyright: Royal Commission on the Ancient and Historical Momuments of Scotland

Between 1973 and 1975 the 25 houses at Hillpark Loan were built (above) and the following year work began on the group of 55 terraced houses and flats arranged around courtyards and called Hillpark Wood. This development was the winner of the N.H.B.C's award for best designed private housing (higher price category) in Scotland in the 1970's

Crown Copyright: Royal Commission on the Ancient and Historical Momuments of Scotland

Hillpark Way (above) and Hillpark Wood (below) as photographed in 2000

Crown Copyright: Royal Commission on the Royal and Ancient Monuments of Scotland

A new luxury development called Hillpark Pines was built in 1989 on what had been previously known locally as the 'marle pits' (see page 106). The new development consisted of 19 large detached houses with the first phase consisting of 3 houses of 6 bedrooms with triple garage (costing £490,000) and 5 of 5 bedrooms and 4 of 4 bedrooms these latter houses having double garages and costing around £360,000.

During the early 1990's recession, the luxury houses were difficult to sell but by 1995 with economic recovery well underway, the estate began to sell much more easily and it won the 1995 'Which House' magazine award.   By May 1996 two more houses were being built and a new show house opening.   Above - prior to the new houses being built and below - after they had been built.

March Gait is another Mactaggart & Mickel housing development in March Road nearing completion. It consists of fourteen 5 bedroom detached villas with double garages and conservatory, see architect's illustration of one villa above, and five 4 bedroomed cottages, see photograph below. All of the houses have been sold.

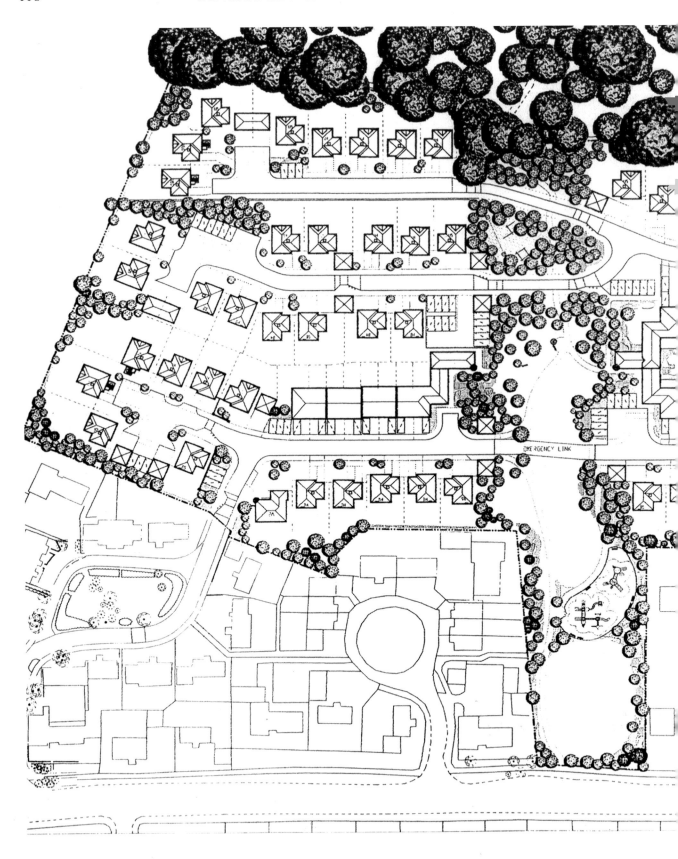

The above is a site layout drawing of Mactaggart and Mickel's newest development which they hope to proceed with early in 2001. It is a fifteen acre site on the Corstorphine Hill beyond the Hillpark Brae, Green and Terrace area on which 162 units will be erected, consisting of 1-2 bedroom flats, 2-3 bedroom bungalows and 4-5 bedroom detached villas.

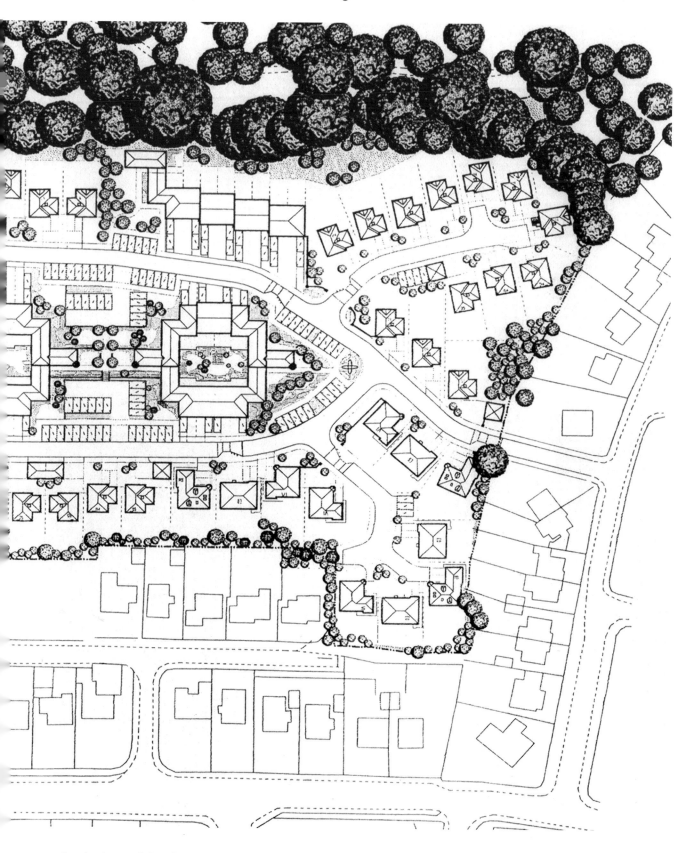

And what of the future? Blackhall is obviously continuing to expand. It is a very pleasant area in which to live and houses are much in demand. Yet despite the growth in population, there remains something of the original community spirit and long may that continue to flourish.

BIBLIOGRAPHY

"Blackhall" by J. Stuart K. Milne

Blackhall School Log Books

Blackhall United Free Church Brochure

"Building Stones of Edinburgh" edited by A. A. McMillan
Published by Edinburgh Geographical Society

Cassels "Old & New Edinburgh"

Census Returns 1841 - 91

Craigcrook Mortification Trust

Craigcrook Estate Records

Edinburgh, An Illustrated Architectural Guide - Charles McKean

Old Maps of Edinburgh

"Place Names of Edinburgh" by Stuart Harris

Ravelston Estate Brochure

Registers of Scotland

Royal Commission on the Royal and Ancient Monuments of Scotland

"Stones & Curiosities of Edinburgh & Neighbourhood"
by George Fothergill

"The Street Names of Edinburgh"
Edited by A. W. Scotland, A. J. Taylor & W. G. Park

Index

A

Adamson, Robert 81
Adamson, William 81

B

Bannatyne, Janet 17
Barnton Terrace 11, 51
Barnton Estate 44 - 77
Belford Gardens 40
Blackhall Athletic Lads 24
Blackhall Bowling Club 21
Blackhall Emporium 52
Blackhall Inn 9
Blackhall Library 76
Blackhall Nursery 29
Blackhall Primary School 64 - 67
Blackhall Recreation Association 14
Blackhall Sports 23
Blackhall Tennis Club 21 - 22
Blackhall United Free Church 72
Blinkbonny Avenue 40
Blinkbonny Crescent 5, 11, 38
Blinkbonny Farm 36
Blinkbonny Road 41
Blinkbonny Terrace 41
Boland & Company Ltd., T. 25
Burns, Robert 54

C

Caie's 6
Cala Homes (Scotland) Ltd. 31
Carfrae Grove 88
Carfrae Park 88
Carfrae Road 88
Columba Avenue 3, 94
Columba Road 11, 12, 80, 93, 94
Constable, Archibald 82
Corstorphine Hill 106, 112
Corstorphine Woods 16
Cottage Park 1
Cottage Park Housing Complex 35
Craggan Cottage 5
Craigcrook Avenue 85, 106
Craigcrook Castle 1, 34, 81, 90
Craigcrook Farm 10, 12, 78, 79, 80, 93
Craigcrook Farm Cottages 3
Craigcrook Gardens 102
Craigcrook Grove 85
Craigcrook Lodge 84
Craigcrook Mortification Trust 81, 88, 92
Craigcrook Park 85
Craigcrook Place 26, 101

Craigcrook Road
10, 11,   33, 34, 79, 87, 103, 106, 108, 111, 112
Craigcrook Square 85
Craigcrook Terrace 6, 101
Craigleith Crescent 43
Craigleith Drive 43
Craigleith Quarry 4, 43 - 48
Craigleith Road 11, 50, 51
Craigleith Shopping Centre 48, 49
Craigleith Station 10, 36, 42
Crest Hotel 37
Croall family 82

D

De Alyncrum, John 78
Dean Estate 36 - 43
Dean Park 36, 37
Denholm, Alexander 1, 7
Denholm Cottage 6, 7
Denholm, Matthew 1
Drylaw Crescent 46, 69
Duncan, Tommy 2
Dunlop, C. H. 39

E

Esso Gararge 37

F

Forthview Road 68
Forthview Terrace 11, 68
Foulis, George 17, 20
Foulis, Sir John 1, 20

G

Gardiner Grove 92
Gardiner, Rev. Dr. 92
Gardiner Road 11, 12, 79, 92
Gardiner Terrace 92
Groathill 47
Groathill Road South 50
Gunpowder Magazine Store 54

H

Henderson's Buildings 2
Hillhouse Road 77
Hillpark Avenue 108, 110
Hillpark Estate 107 - 119
Hillpark Loan 113
Hillpark Pines 115
Hillpark Way 114
Hillpark Wood 113, 114
Hillview 74
Hillview Crescent 62
Hillview Road 59, 68

Hillview Terrace 3, 11, 59
Holiday Inn 37
House O' Hill 5
House o' Hill Avenue 71
House o' Hill Dairy 3, 56
House o' Hill Public House 9
Hunter, John 82

J

Jeffrey Avenue 11, 90
Jeffrey, Lord 82, 90

K

Keith, Alexander 4, 20
Keith Crescent 103
Keith Murray, Sir Patrick 20
Keith Row 10, 26, 27, 57
Keith Row, Terrace and Crescent. 16
Keith Terrace 28

L

Leper., John 78
Loch Road 106

M

Mactaggart & Mickel 106
Maidencraig 47
Maidencraig Court 53
Maidencraig Crescent 54
Maidencraig Farm 5, 53
Maidencraig Quarry 54
Maidencraig Villa 56
March Gait 117
March Road 89, 106
Marischal Place 3, 4, 16
Marle Pits 106
Mary Erskine School for Girls. 25
McGregor Chalmers, Mr. P. 95
Millar and Son, James 39
More of Abercorn, Sir William 17
Muir, A., 8
Muirdale Terrace 8
Murray Gartshore, Colonel 20
Murray Gartshore Memorial Hall 3, 14
Murray Gartshore, Miss 14,16, 20, 21, 24
Murrayfield Golf Club 21

O

Orchard Park 39

P

Park Cottage 34
Paton, Russel 1
Primrose, Sir Alexander 20
Primrose, Sir Archibald 20

Q

Queen's Avenue 11, 60, 61
Queen's Avenue South 62

Queen's Court. 66
Queen's Crescent 64
Queen's Road 62
Queensferry Road 1, 8, 36, 39, 77,106,108,111

R

Ravelston Dykes 36, 39
Ravelston Estate 14 - 35
Ravelston Garden 12
Ravelston Golf Club 22
Ravelston House 4, 17, 24, 25
Ravelston Lodge 15
Ravelston Park 23, 24, 29, 30
Ravelston Quarries 32
Ravelston Woods 79
Ravleston Dykes Road 33

S

Sainsbury Superstore 47 - 50
Scott, Sir Walter 20
Scout Field 30
Seaforth Drive 59
Seaforth Terrace 3
Simpson, James 56
Simpson's Dairy 26, 56, 101
St. Columba's Church 8, 11, 78, 95 - 100
St. Cuthbert's Cooperative Society 52
Stevenson, Rev. W.B. 95
Stewart Clark, Mrs. 24, 25
Strachan Gardens 87
Strachan House 87
Strachan, John 81
Strachan Road 12, 86

T

Telford Road 12, 46, 70, 75
Thain Building 9
The Rec Magazine 14

V

Viewpoint Sheltered Housing Development 55
Village Coachworks and Garage. 2

W

Ware's Stores 9
West Barnton Terrace 11, 51
Whitehall Garage 75